To all the sad folk

Hang in there, it gets better. Use these words to help guide you through your own journey, know that you aren't alone and there are so many others that feel the same way you do. So, I put them into words and pictures, so you can remind yourself of this.

Diagnosis

Why does this feel like a death sentence?
I wanted an answer, but that's all I wanted.
Why does this feel like a dark cloud
hanging over me?
Like it's raining over everything?
Rain should help the flowers grow,
but it's drowning them instead.

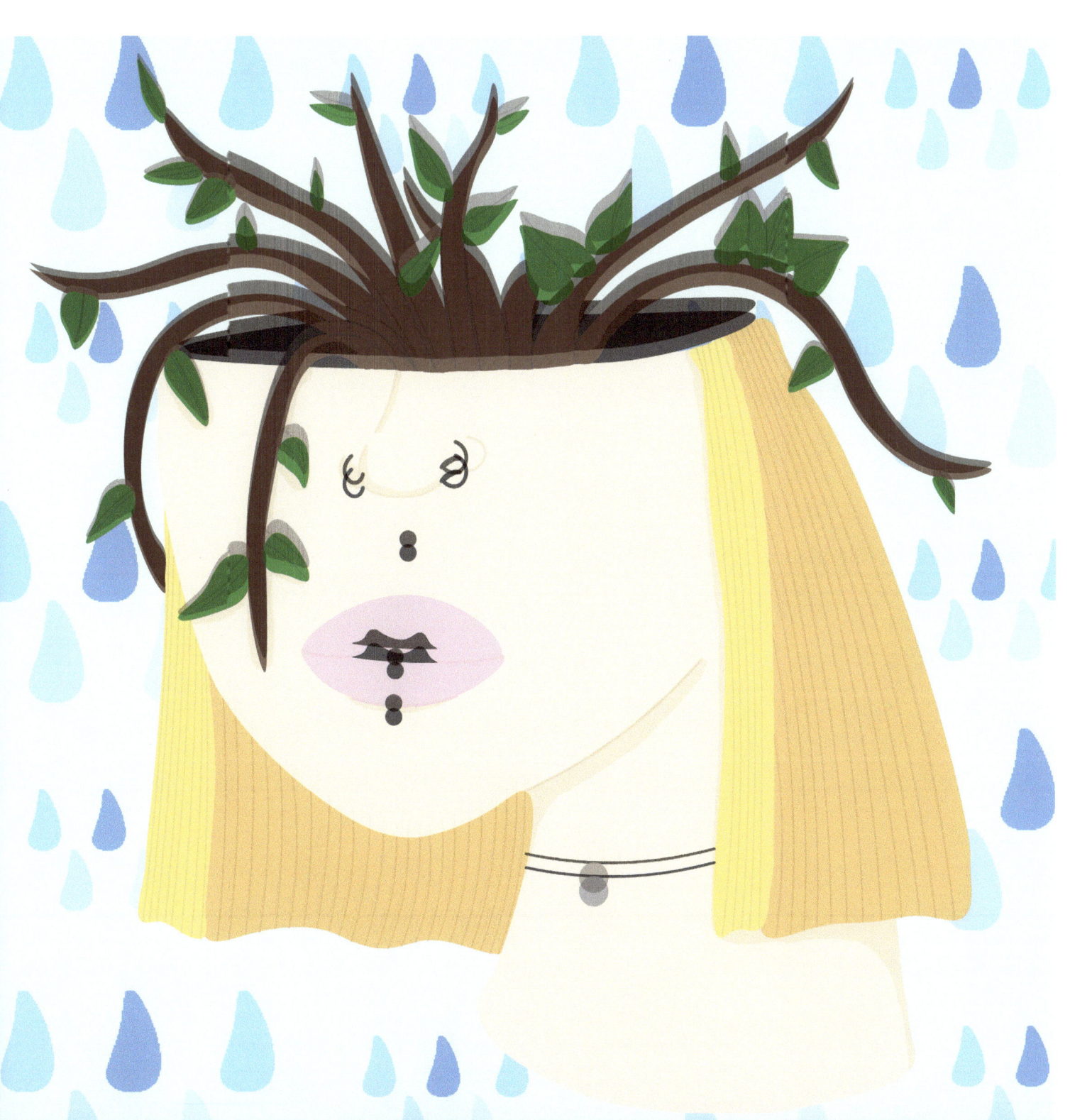

Underwater

Come with me to the bottom of the sea,
swim with me to the ocean's depth
to a place where I have nothing left.
I can't feel the waves crashing,
there's only emptiness.
It seems my ship abandoned me,
I'm anchored to this feeling,
and I've forgotten how to swim.
I hope someone up there remembers me,
as I drown underwater at the bottom of the sea.

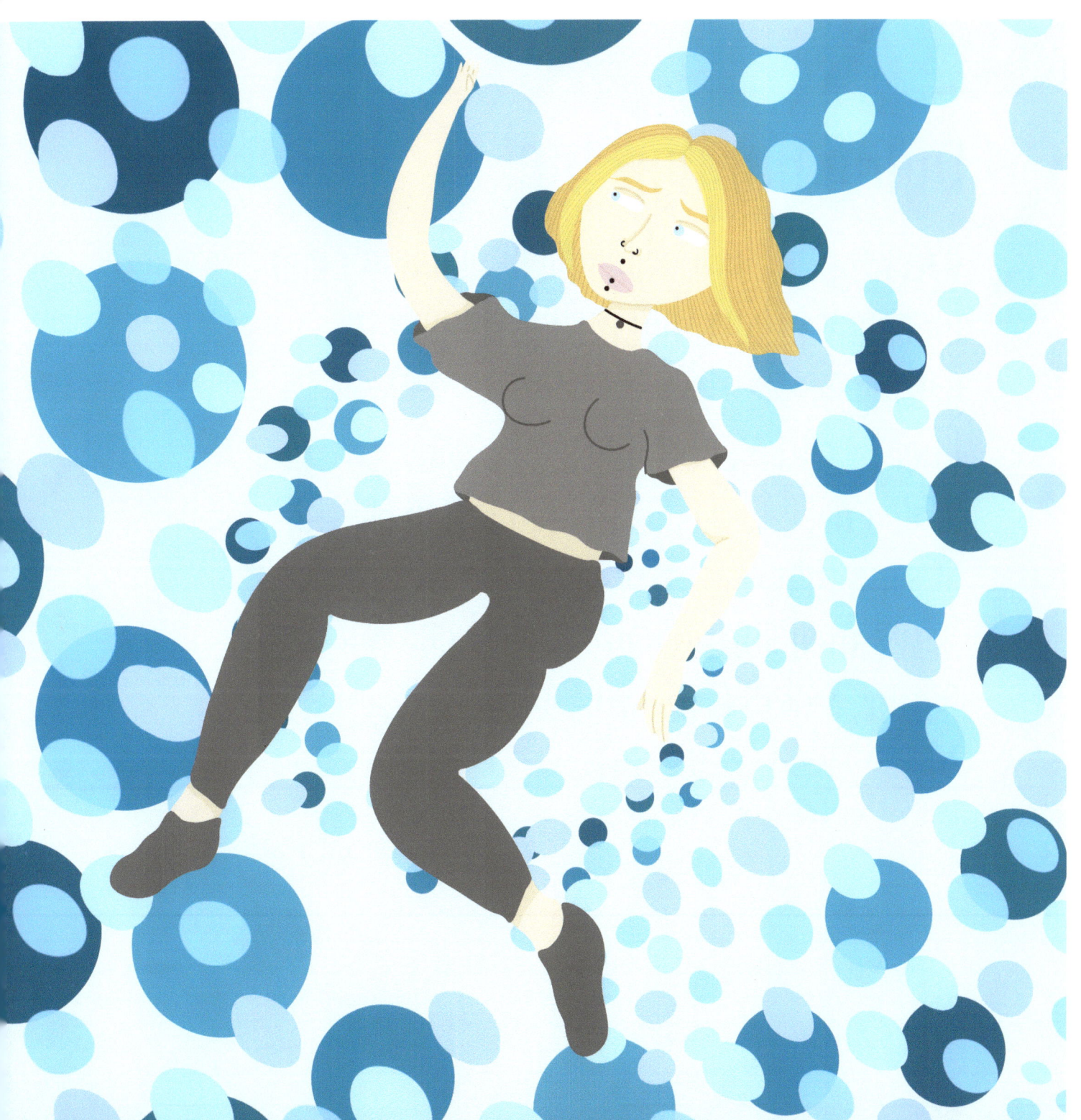

Dying my hair pink

Recently I've been thinking of dying my hair pink, and I think that means things are getting worse.

I need excitement, I fancy a change, or do I need to feel as though I'm in control of something?

Rose tinted glasses don't seem to be working for me, so I'm giving this a try.

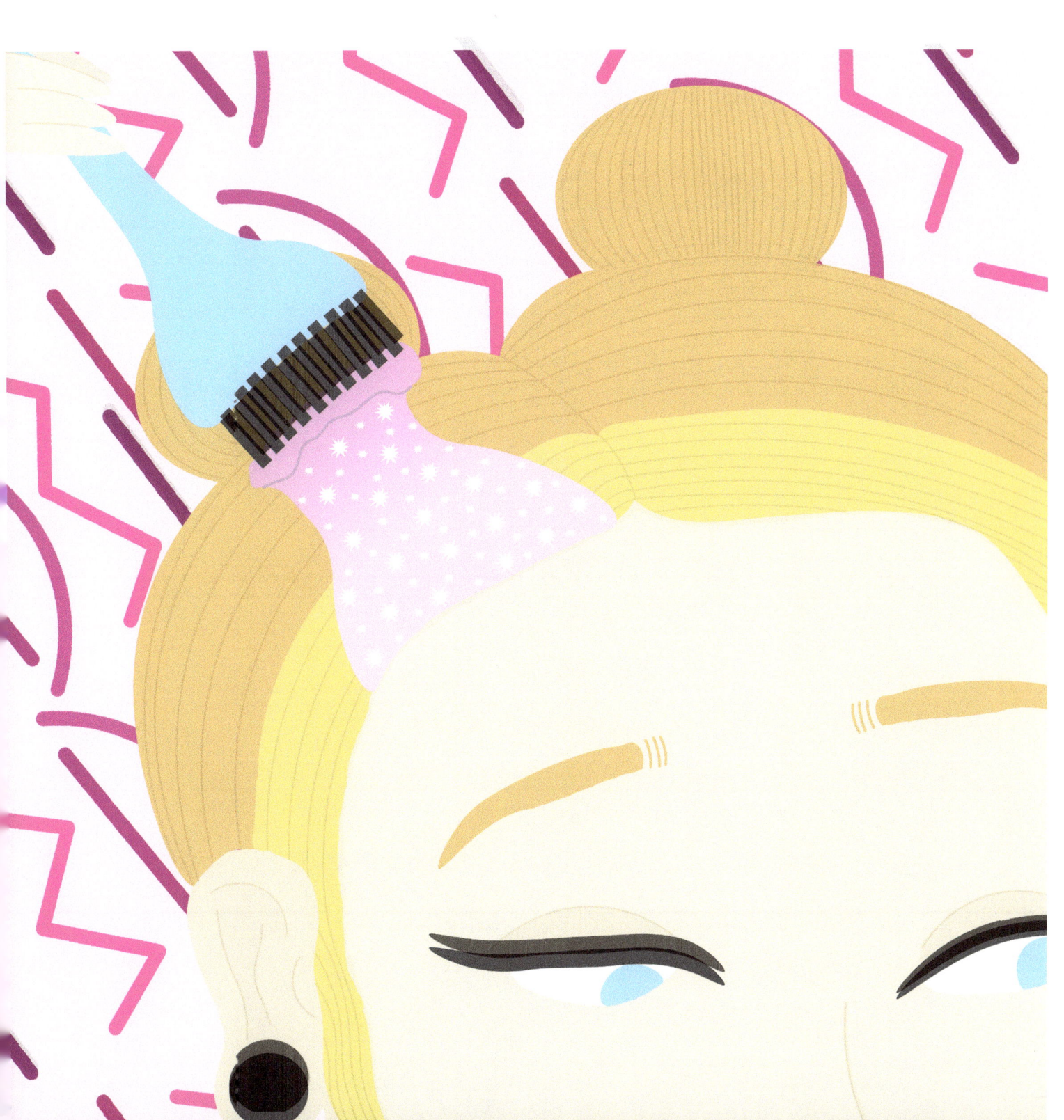

Pretty

The first time someone told me I was fat I was five,
and this would continue through the rest of my life.
Pretty for a fat girl, but not as pretty as the rest.
Pretty for the weird girl, but never able to impress.
Somehow, I'm just never enough,
there seems something in me that's too difficult to love.
Maybe these feelings are better left in my past,
I must improve and adapt so I can build a life for myself.

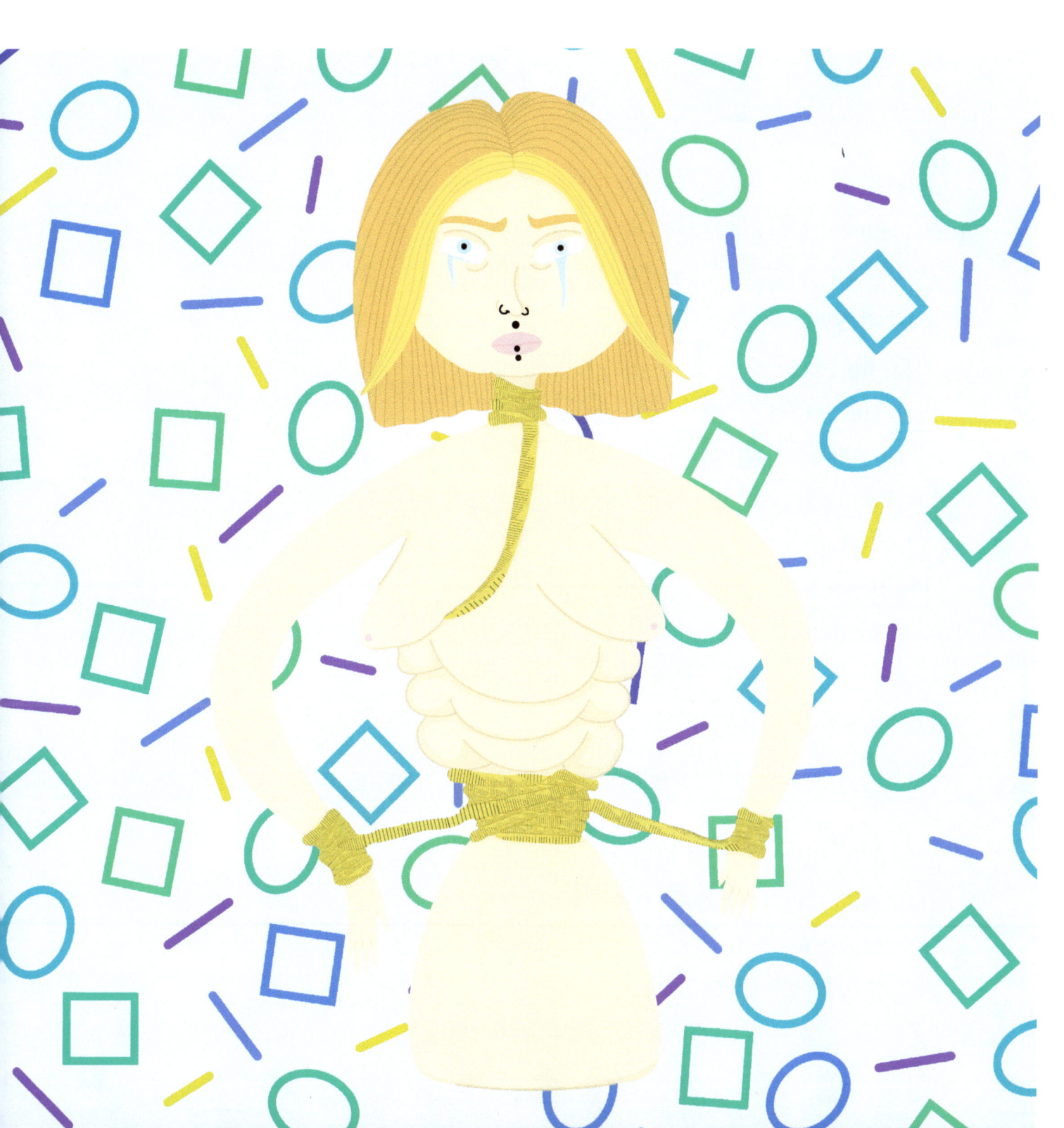

Boys

Why do boys do anything they do?
It's like they think being male is a free pass to do whatever they want.
What makes you think I want your opinion on my body? I don't remember asking for it.
Please come up with a better way to impress me than your back handed compliments or a picture of your dick.
"Pretty for a big girl" isn't a compliment.
I don't care if I'm "not like other girls".
And neither do my friends, or the Instagram models you follow.
Honestly, why do you talk at all?

But then I guess not all boys are bad, in the same way not all girls are bitches.
Somewhere I bet there are boys wondering why girls do anything they do.

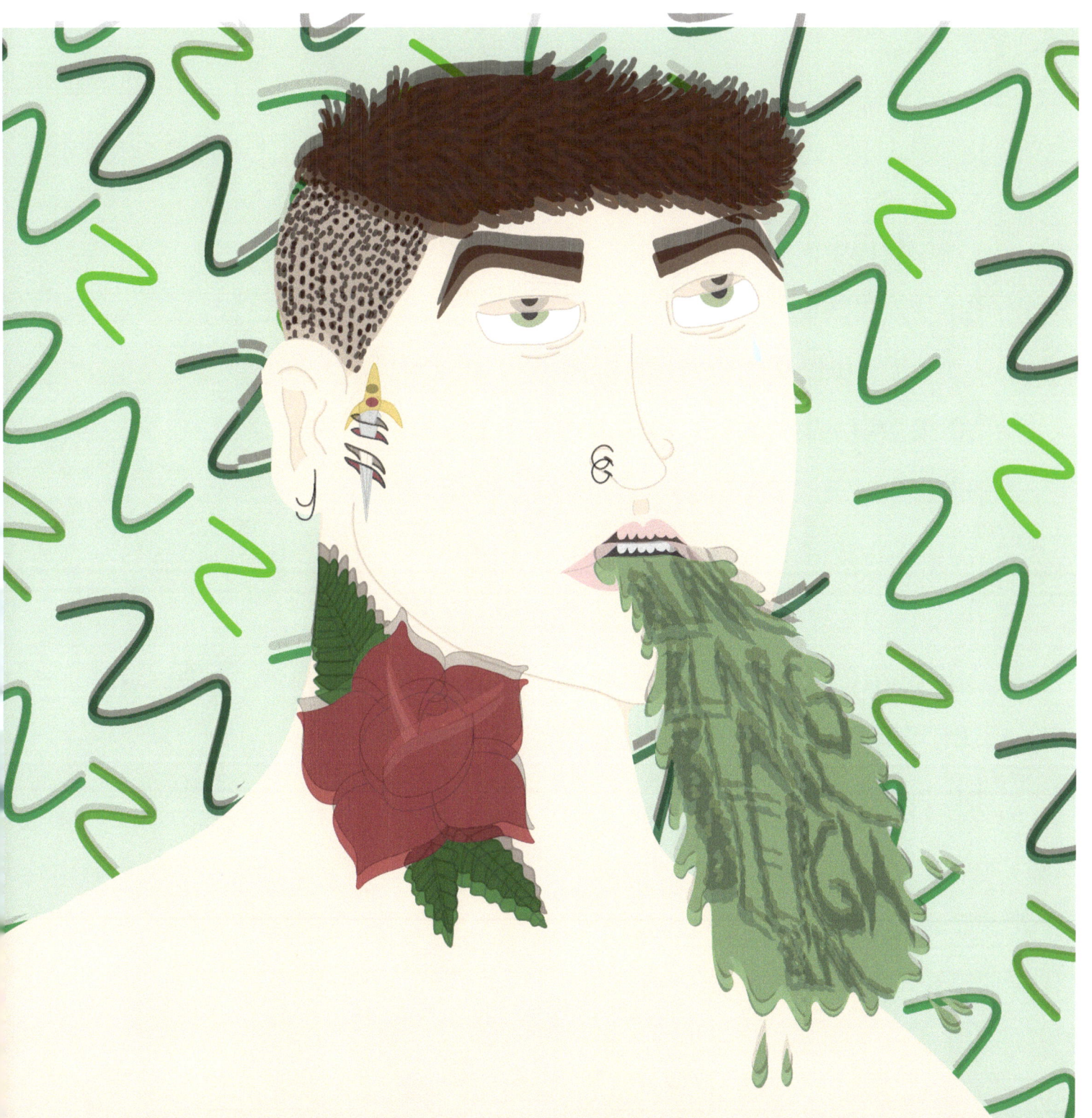

L

I held you on a pedestal so high, how could I not expect you to fall?
I loved you so much, but I never felt it back.
So many wishes left ungranted, all your promises are empty.
You made me feel like I wasn't enough, but there were more than me.
Someone old, someone new,
someone else's, a much whiter shade of blue.

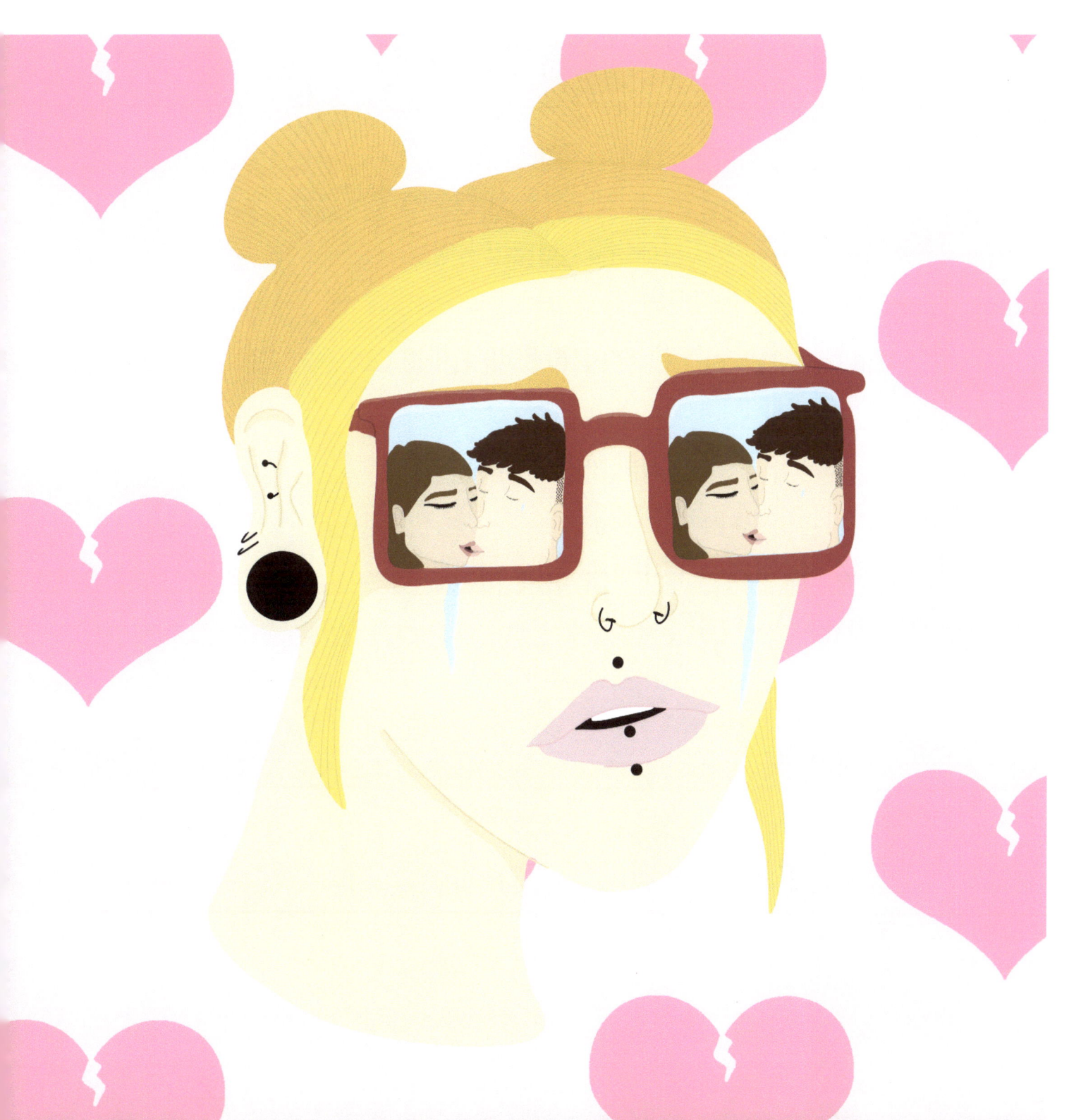

The Princess

There is a princess in a tower, and I must keep her locked away;
It's the only choice I have, the only thing that keeps her safe;
She's sweet and kind and pure of heart, she's precious in every way;
That's why this tower is the only place for her, outside just isn't safe.

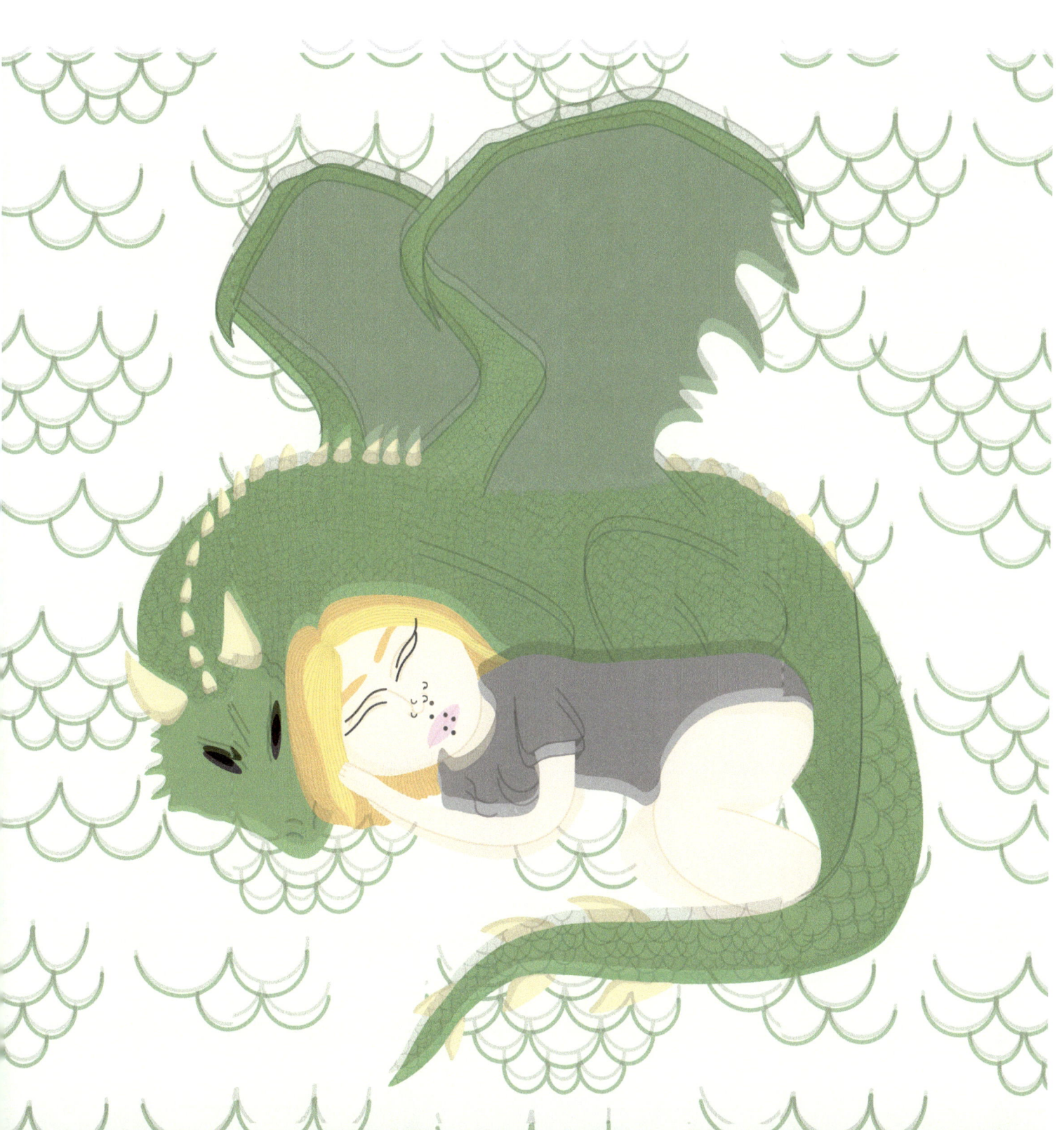

Mansplaining

When you feel the need to explain something to me, don't.
Although you think my tiny lady brain can't understand, it can.
I don't need you to explain this to me, I can work it out for myself.
While I'm speaking could you not cut me off?
Especially just to tell me about more stuff i must be too stupid to grasp the concept of,
As I was born a girl it must feel like a duty to you, can you mansplain that for me?

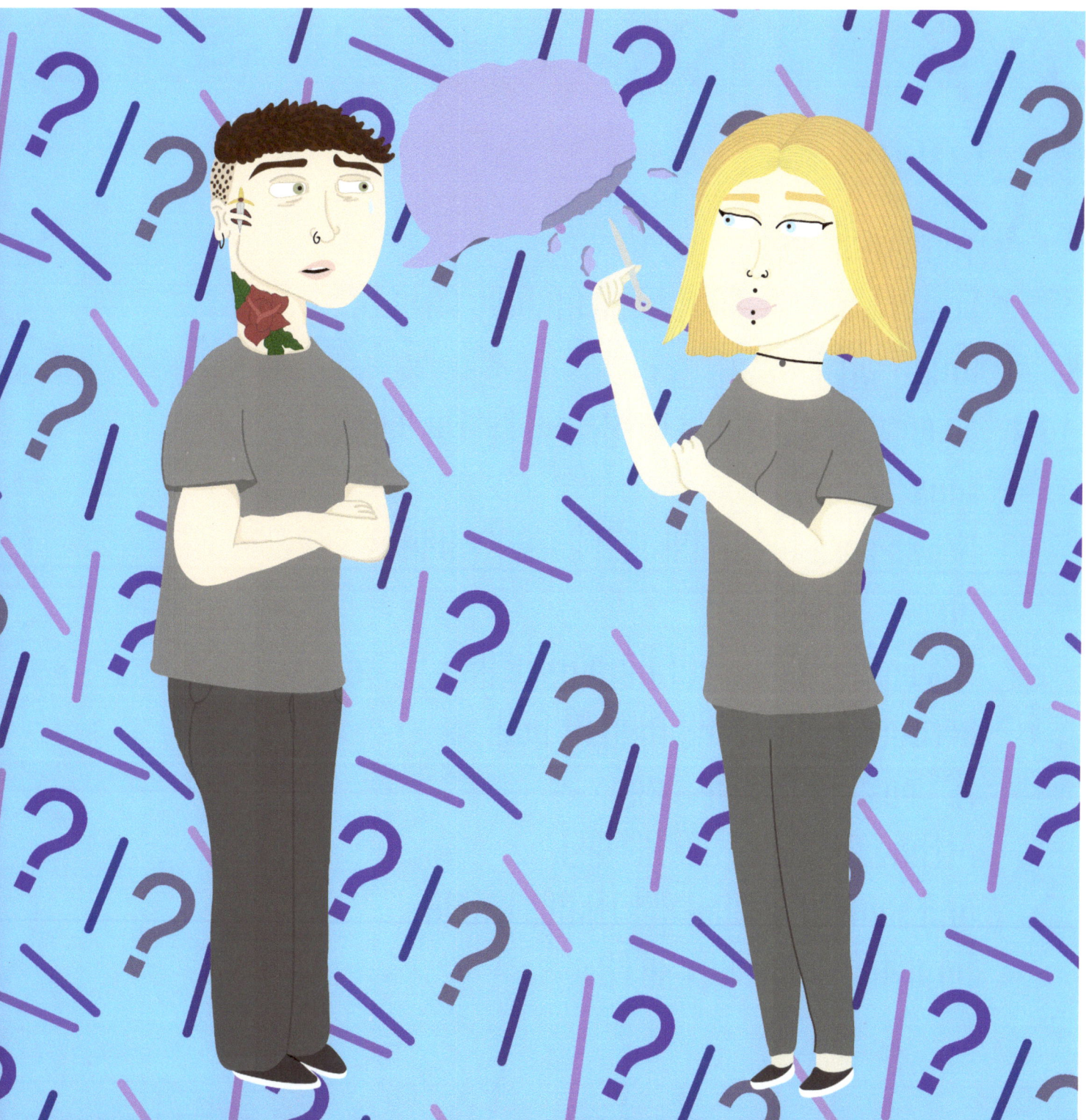

Easy

You are so easy:
Easy to talk to, easy to be around, easy to laugh with.
So easy to get along with, and everybody says it.
It's so easy to fall for you because you're just so likeable.
It's easy losing an argument to you because I can't stay mad at you.
It's easy to forgive you.
Although you're not perfect,
and sometimes you get things wrong,
forgiving you is just so easy.

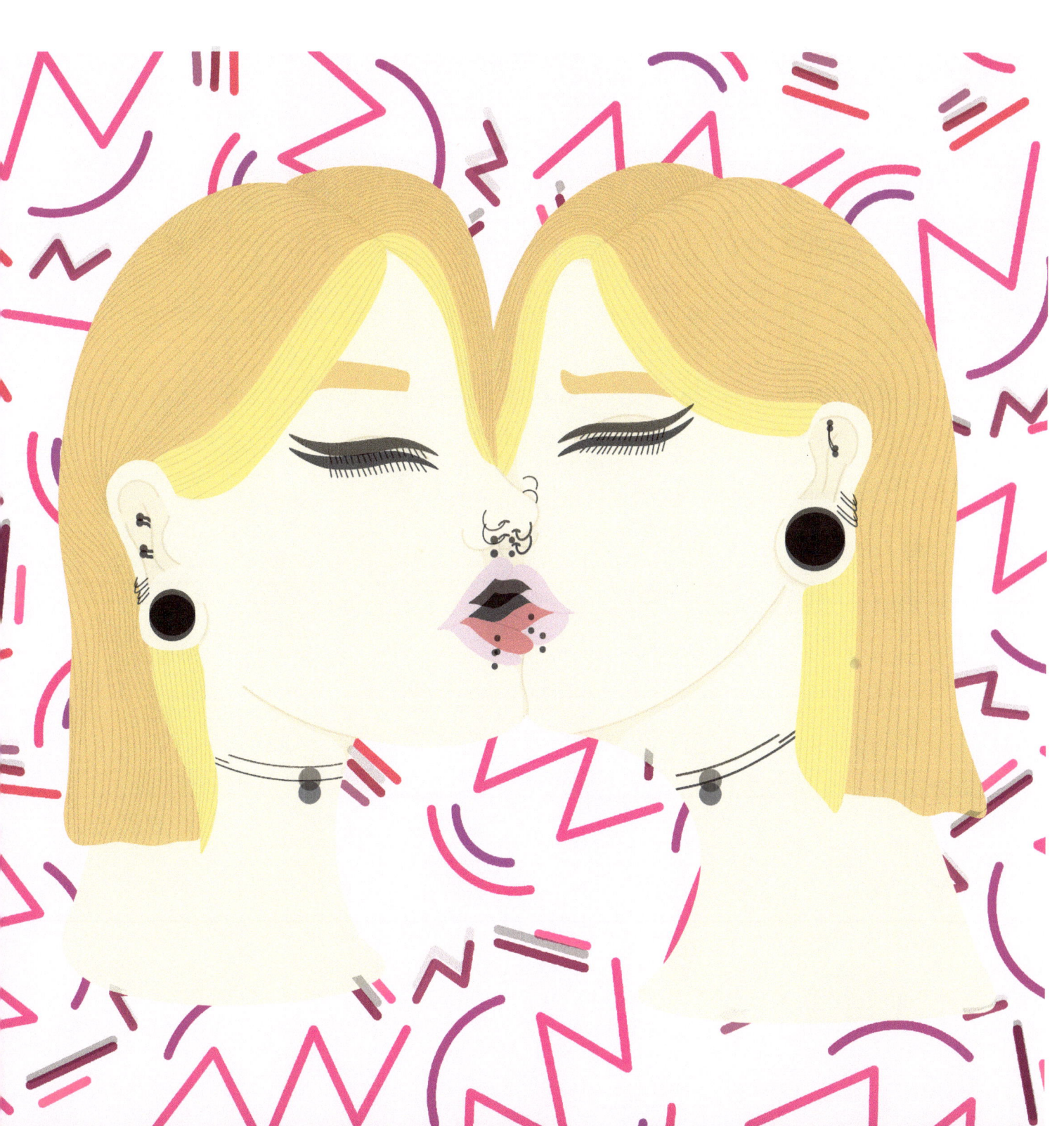

To my nineteen-year-old self

I see the pain you're in, I know how much you're struggling,
and I need you to know it's going to be fine.
You'll be happy in the end; you don't believe me but it's true.
You're going to be so fucking happy.
You're going to be so loved by so many people.
It gets better, you get better.
You're going to be amazed by what you can achieve.
You're going to find love again; you'll find it in yourself first.
You're going to be broken, but you'll build yourself back up again.
Keep going, because it's going to be worth it.

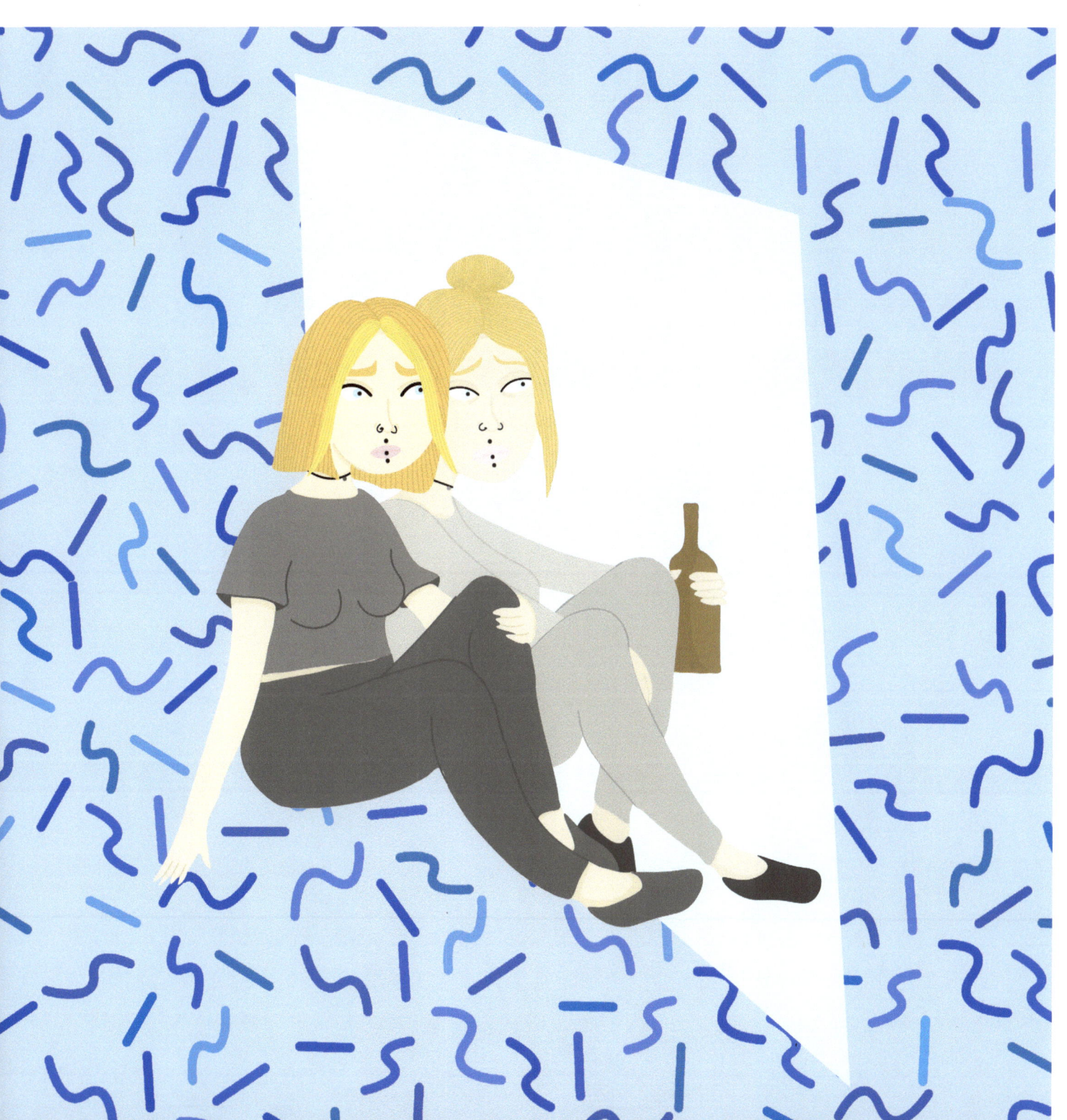

Dedications

To my friends; Thank you for your love, kindness and never-ending support. You keep me going.
To the boys; Thank you for inspiring these poems, try to stay out of them in future.
To Meg; I love you, keep creating, keep writing, be bold, stay strong.

Author

Meg Dobson-Armstrong is a budding creative from the north east of England, her work encompasses a range of social issues, the struggles of daily life living with mental illness, relationships and everything in-between with a sense of humour and witt that will make you smile.

www.ingramcontent.com/pod-product-compliance
Lightning Source LLC
Chambersburg PA
CBHW051944210526
45473CB00006B/2372